COMPOSER SHOWCASE
HAL LEONARD STUDENT PIANO LIBRARY

Lyric Ballads

SIX ROMANTIC PIECES FOR PIANO SOLO

BY CHRISTOS TSITSAROS

CONTENTS

T0057886

ISBN 978-1-4768-1327-1

HAL•LEONARD®
CORPORATION

7777 W. BLUEMOUND RD. P.O. BOX 13819 MILWAUKEE, WI 53213

In Australia Contact:
Hal Leonard Australia Pty. Ltd.
4 Lentara Court
Cheltenham, Victoria, 3192 Australia
Email: ausadmin@halleonard.com.au

Visit Hal Leonard Online at
www.halleonard.com

Performance Notes

To those who are blessed with the gift of love or who hope for love.

Album Leaf

Originally conceived in E-flat minor, the earlier version of this piece featured a flowing accompaniment in sixteenth notes. While re-working the piece for this collection, I discovered that a rhythmically simpler accompaniment is just as expressive if not more, in that it adds to the languishing character of the music and puts the main melodic lines in a more prominent spot.

The pleading dialogue in the beginning phrases is followed by a long lyrical line that progressively grows in intensity and culminates in mm. 13-14. The second section is a variation of the first, with more interaction of the tenor and a few rhythmic changes that add to the permeating pathos and expressivity. Experiment with various degrees of *rubato* in an overall slow but flexible tempo. Demonstrate convincingly the dramatic arc of the long phrase, letting it resolve in the undefined, questioning phrases.

Love Song in the Rain

The soft rustle of forest leaves serves as a background drop to this gentle love song. The section in the relative major, more driven and luminous, speaks of happiness, abandon, and surrender. Maintain a steady, flowing tempo, never allowing the left hand to overpower the melody. The use of the soft pedal where indicated will enhance the appropriate tone differentiation: a somewhat softer color suitable for the outer sections, and a brighter, more generous tone for the middle section.

Morning Tenderness

This sensual piece is about the warm, tender feeling of inner tranquility, gratitude for life, and love for the ones who make a difference in our lives. It is about being content in our existence and having faith in the benevolence of the world. Play the first part in a sustained, slow tempo, lavishing each phrase and feeling the subtle chord changes. In the middle section, maintain a rather steady pace and by means of a gradual increase in dynamic and tempo, communicate a sense of perspective, depth, and expectancy. In mm. 33-40, relish the ever-rising waves of sound with enthusiasm and passion. Upon reaching the *tempo commodo* section, keep appeasing until the end. Finally, allow the disarming sweetness of the last harmony infiltrate your entire being.

Night Reflections

Fleeting visions, long avenues, flashing lights, the city enveloped by the dark veil of the night. This abstract, atmospheric piece is based on a stepwise descending harmonic progression with short motivic fragments interspersed here and there. The sixteenth-note variation leads to a more impassioned section that grows in intensity and culminates in mm.33-36. Whenever the two hands play interchangeably in close proximity, it is helpful to match the right hand to the left rather than the opposite. To this effect, keep the left hand steady and even throughout; moreover, do not let the syncopated right-hand rhythm slow down the pace. This can be better achieved by thinking of the syncopated notes as if they were almost played together with the eighth notes of the left hand.

Rays of Hope

This short piece evokes those blessed moments when we find and recognize hope in nature: the chirping of a bird, the first sunrays on a crisp spring day, and the immensity of the sky. The opening short phrases are to be played with suppleness, lightness and spontaneity, almost like an improvisation. Relish the long *cantabile* lines with emotional commitment and inner joy. Writing this piece was an exhilarating experience; in tracing its contours, I became quickly absorbed by this irresistibly uplifting melody. It is so liberating when one finally learns to recognize hope in little things.

Sea Breezes

The inspiration for this piece came to me many years ago, when as a young student I worked for an entire summer playing the piano at the Grand Hotel on Mackinac Island. While being mesmerized by the fascinating rippling effects of Lake Huron, I mentally heard this melody sung by a choir of voices in the midst of the lush afternoon colors and the whisper of the early fall breezes. The pleading song captivated the heart of the observer. As such, play this music with freedom and feeling, following the indicated tempo changes and enlivening the phrasing with progressive dynamic fluctuations, tasteful *rubato*, and sensitive use of the pedal.

*A special note of thanks to Jennifer Linn for her encouragement
and support throughout my career.*

–Christos Tsitsaros

Album Leaf

By Christos Tsitsaros

Molto andante e cantabile

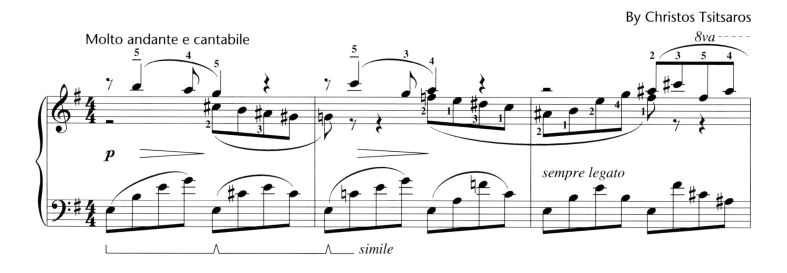

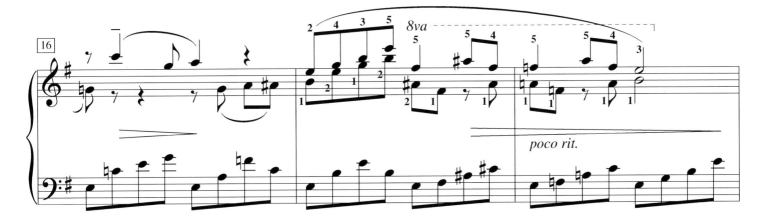

Morning Tenderness

By Christos Tsitsaros

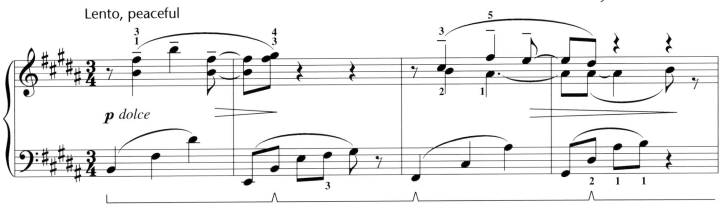

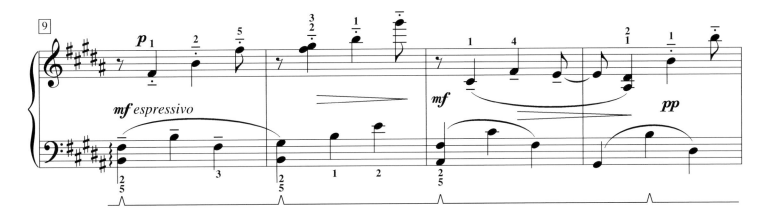

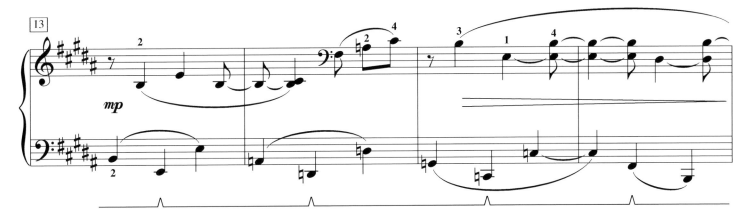

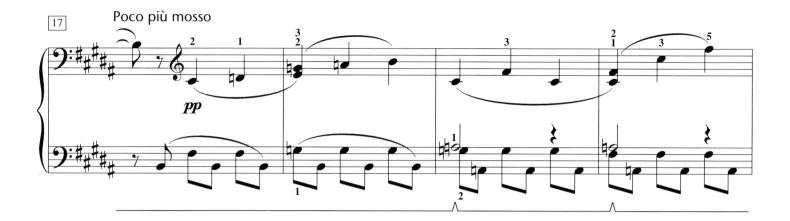

Poco più mosso

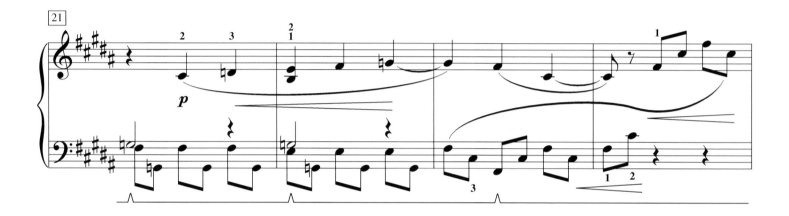

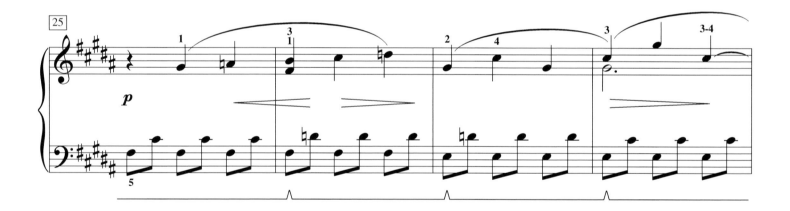

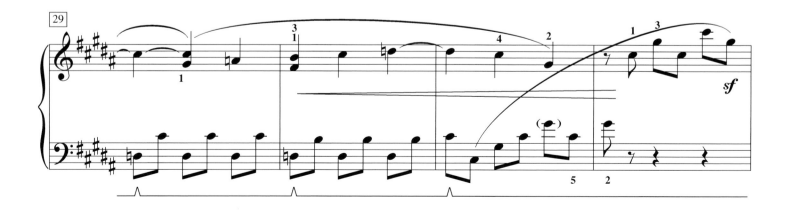

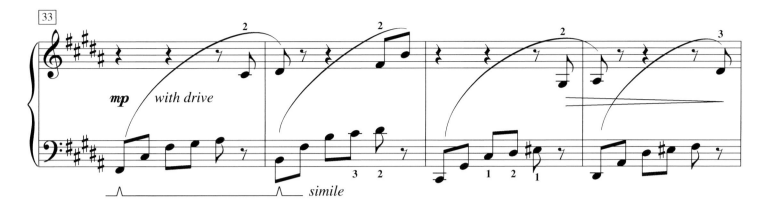

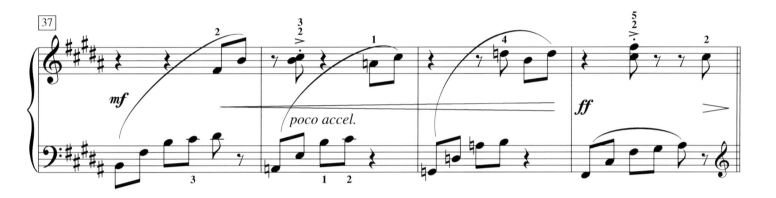

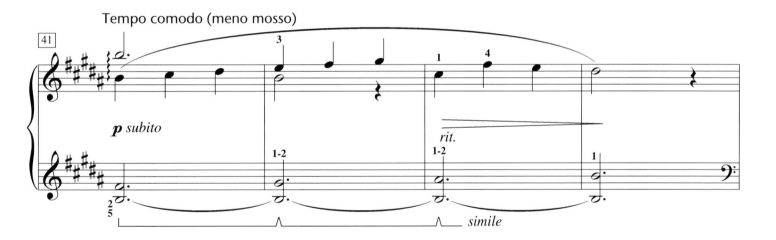

Love Song in the Rain

By Christos Tsitsaros

Allegretto moderato

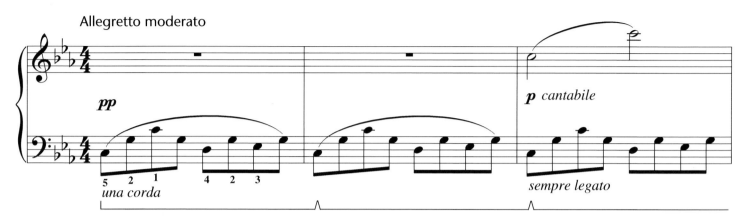

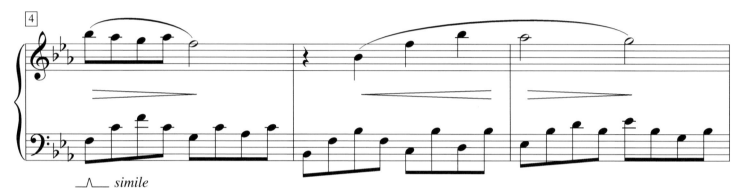

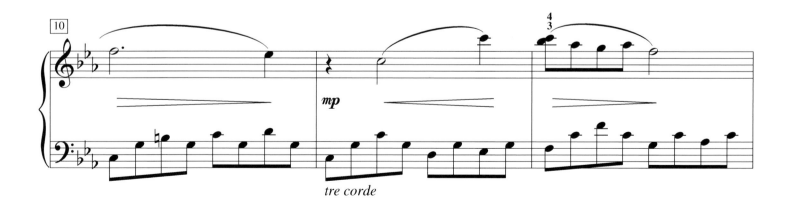

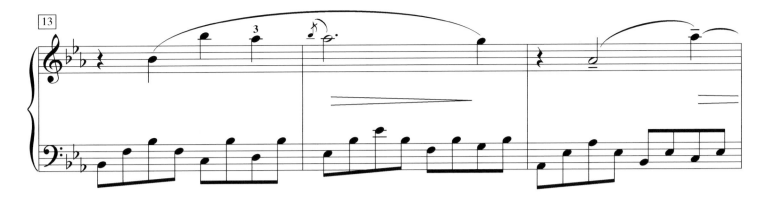

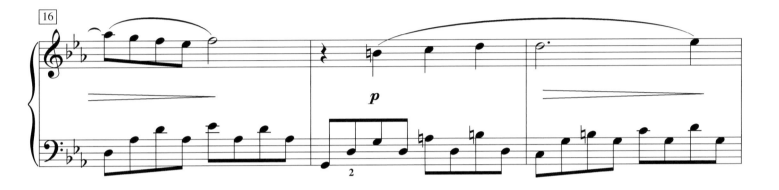

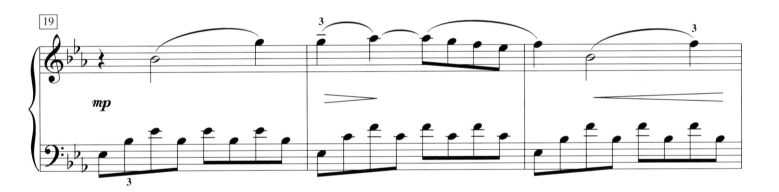

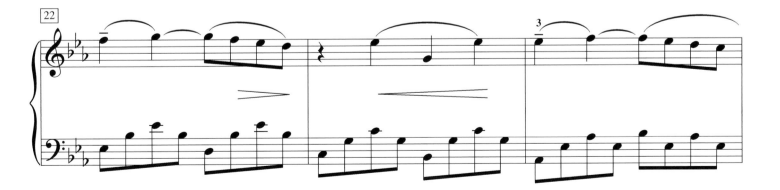

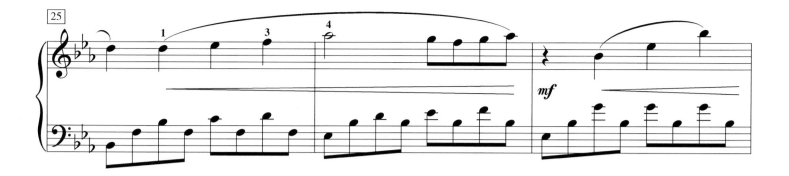

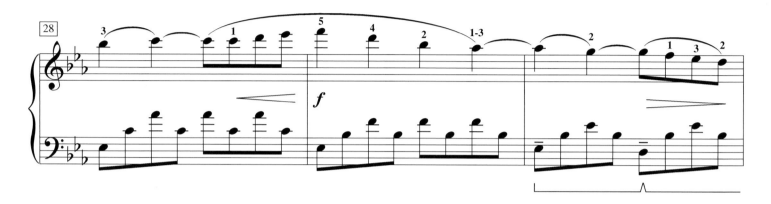

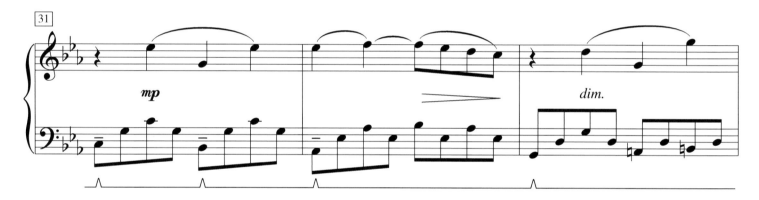

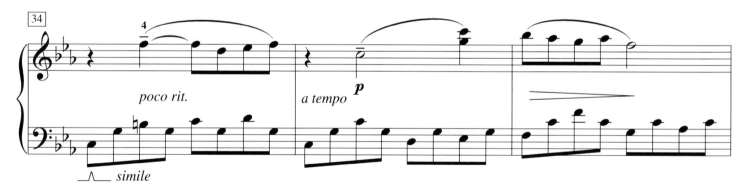

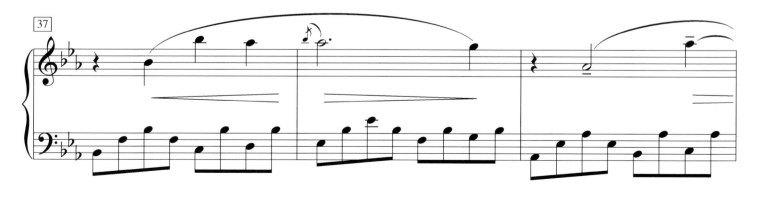

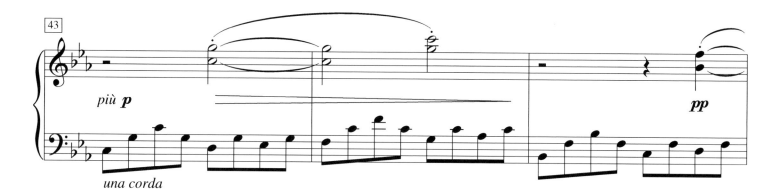

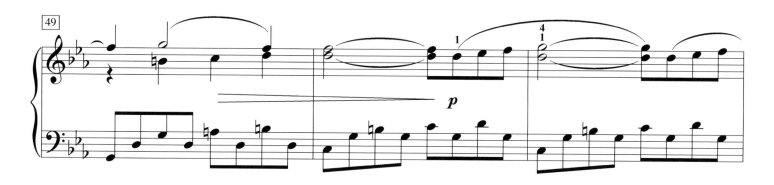

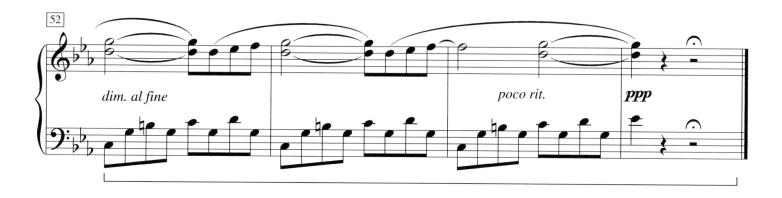

Night Reflections

Allegro moderato, hauntingly

By Christos Tsitsaros

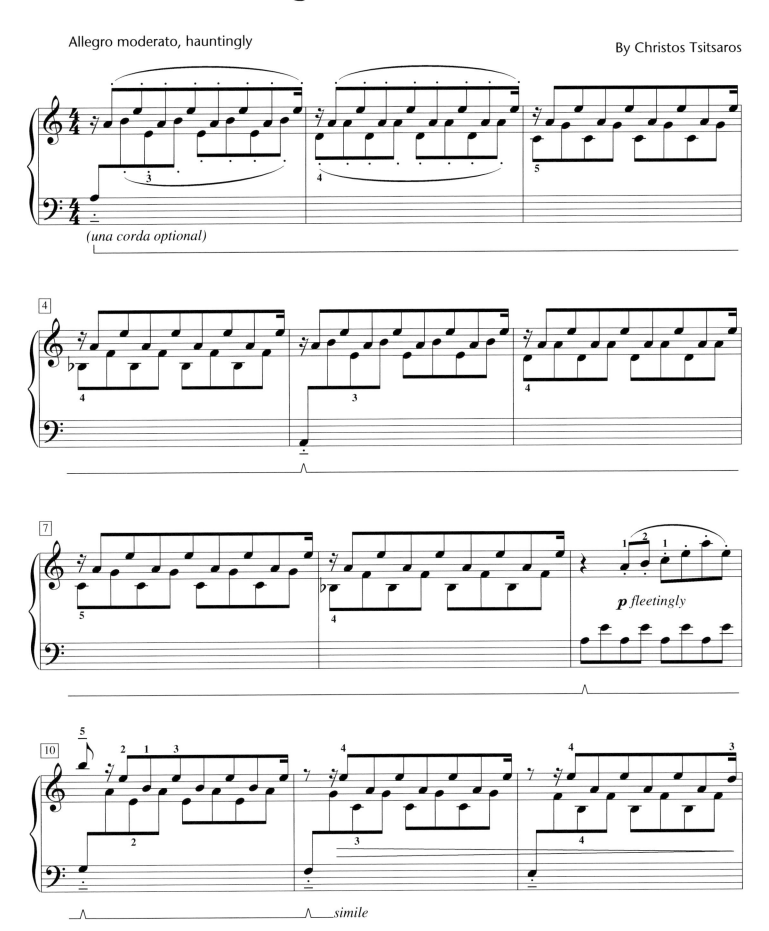

(una corda optional)

p fleetingly

simile

(tre corde)

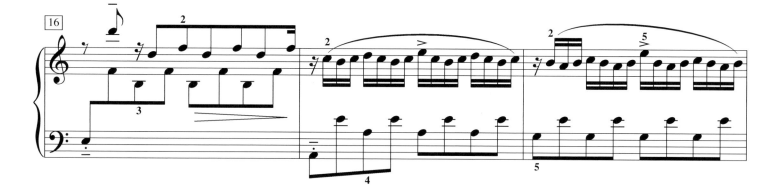

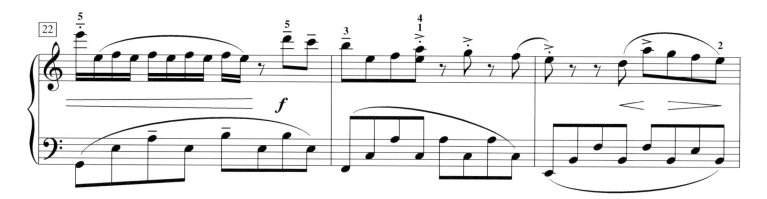

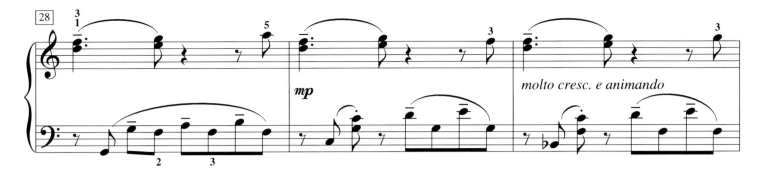

Tempo più mosso

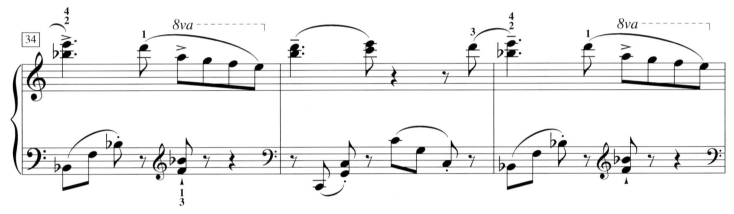

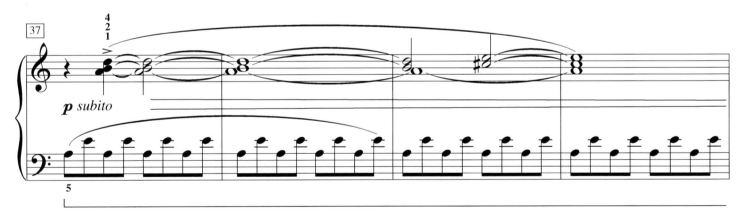

Tempo primo

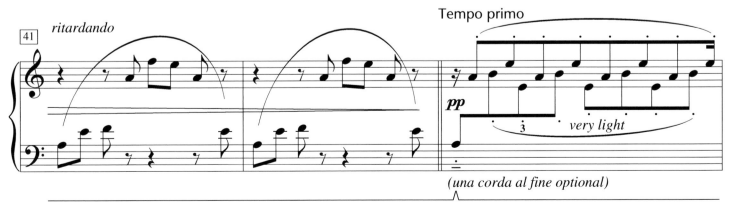

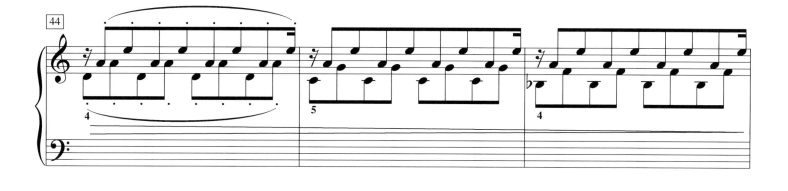

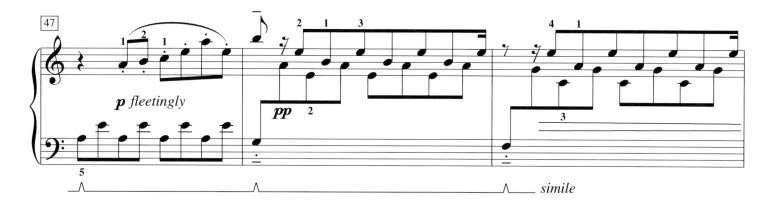

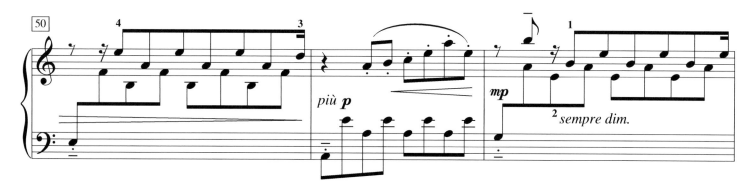

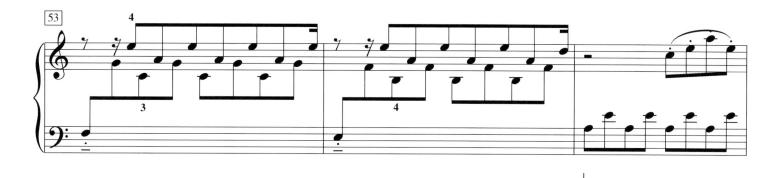

Sea Breezes

By Christos Tsitsaros

Moderato, with motion and freedom

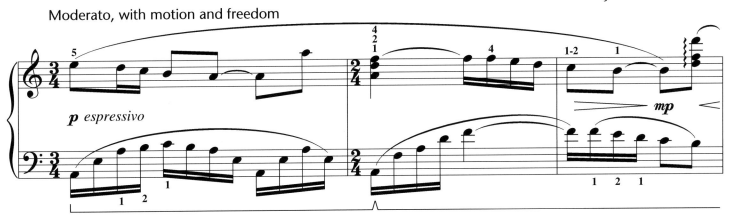

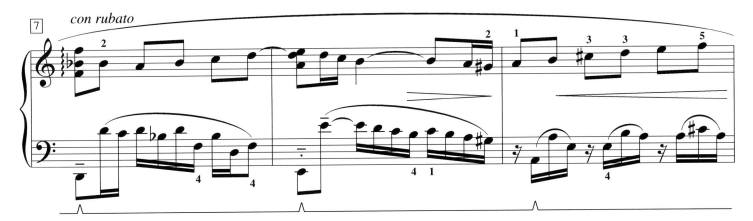

A tempo poco più vivo

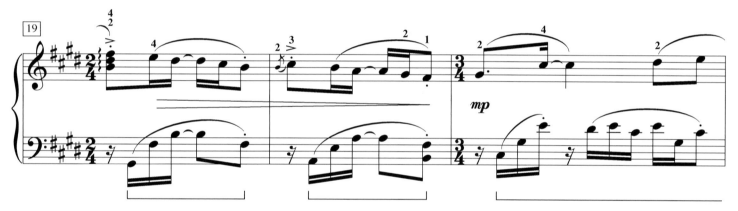

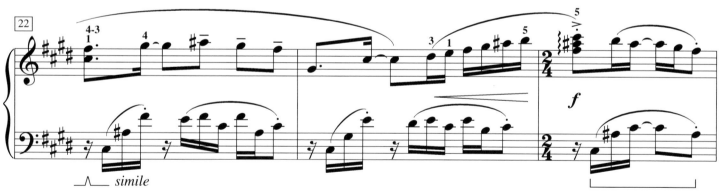

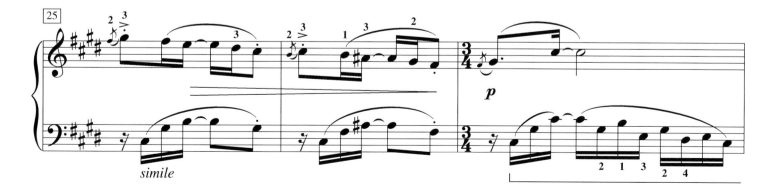

19

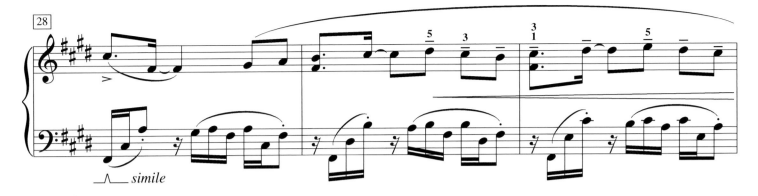

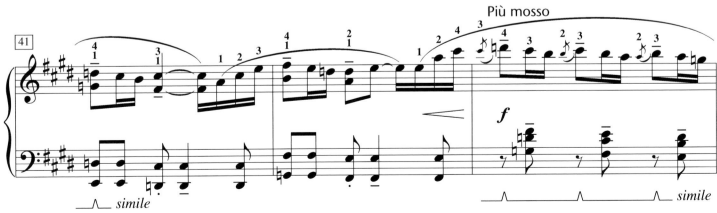

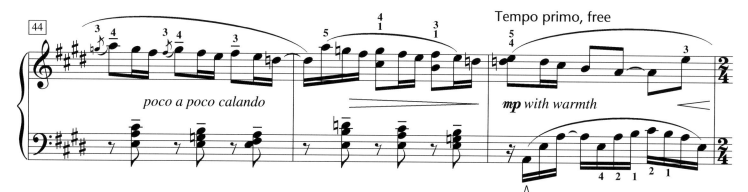

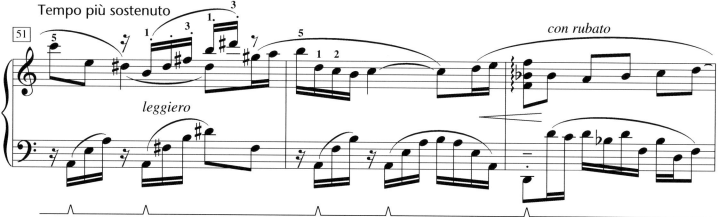

Rays of Hope

By Christos Tsitsaros

Allegretto con moto

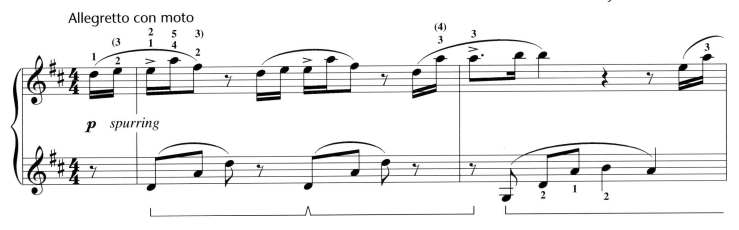

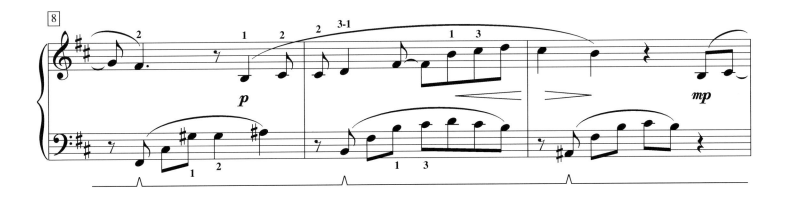

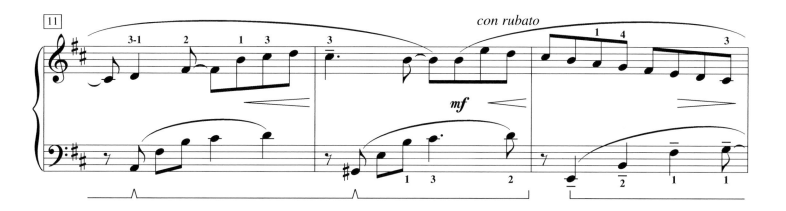

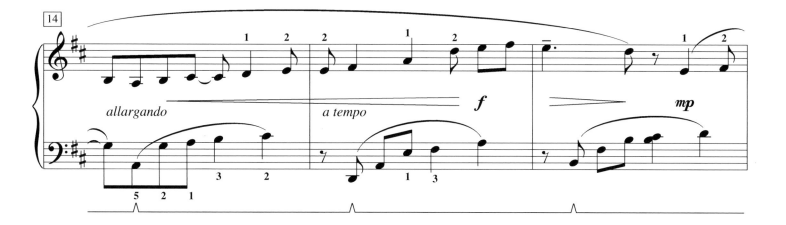

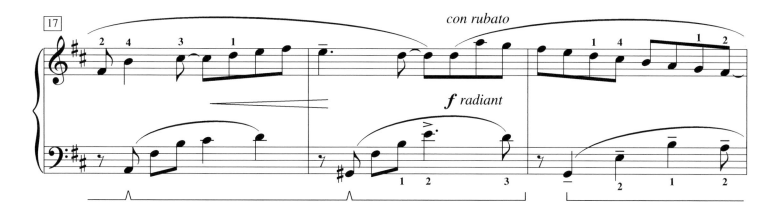

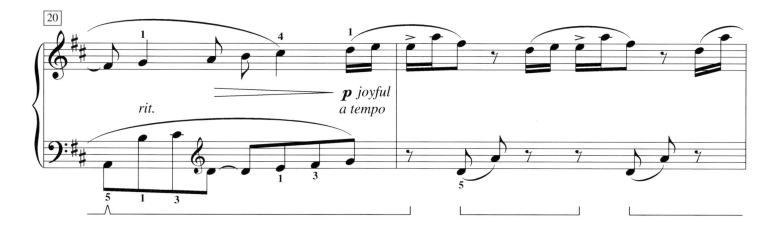